<table>
<tr><td colspan="2" align="center">Personal Information</td></tr>
<tr><td>Name:</td><td>Date of Birth:</td></tr>
<tr><td colspan="2">Adress:</td></tr>
<tr><td colspan="2"></td></tr>
<tr><td colspan="2">Business Adress:</td></tr>
<tr><td colspan="2"></td></tr>
<tr><td colspan="2">Email:</td></tr>
<tr><td colspan="2">Mobile Telephone:</td></tr>
<tr><td colspan="2">Home Telephone:</td></tr>
<tr><td colspan="2">Fax:</td></tr>
</table>

<table>
<tr><td colspan="2" align="center">Emergency Contact</td></tr>
<tr><td>Name:</td><td>Relationship:</td></tr>
<tr><td colspan="2">Adress:</td></tr>
<tr><td colspan="2"></td></tr>
<tr><td colspan="2"></td></tr>
<tr><td colspan="2"></td></tr>
<tr><td colspan="2">Mobile Telephone:</td></tr>
<tr><td colspan="2">Home Telephone:</td></tr>
<tr><td colspan="2">Email:</td></tr>
</table>

<table>
<tr><td align="center">Notes</td></tr>
<tr><td></td></tr>
<tr><td></td></tr>
<tr><td></td></tr>
<tr><td></td></tr>
<tr><td></td></tr>
<tr><td></td></tr>
</table>

<table>
<tr><td colspan="2" align="center">Vehicle Information</td></tr>
<tr><td>Vehicle:</td><td>Year:</td></tr>
<tr><td colspan="2">Make:</td></tr>
<tr><td colspan="2">Model:</td></tr>
<tr><td colspan="2">Engine:</td></tr>
<tr><td colspan="2">VIN Number:</td></tr>
<tr><td>Purchase Date:</td><td>Mileage at Purchase:</td></tr>
<tr><td colspan="2">Purchase Form:</td></tr>
</table>

<table>
<tr><td colspan="2" align="center">Insurance Company</td></tr>
<tr><td colspan="2">Company Name:</td></tr>
<tr><td colspan="2">Adress:</td></tr>
<tr><td colspan="2"></td></tr>
<tr><td>Office:</td><td>Work:</td></tr>
<tr><td>Phone:</td><td>Fax:</td></tr>
<tr><td colspan="2">Email:</td></tr>
<tr><td colspan="2">Website:</td></tr>
<tr><td>Agent:</td><td>Phone:</td></tr>
<tr><td colspan="2">Cost:</td></tr>
<tr><td colspan="2">Insurance Numbre:</td></tr>
<tr><td colspan="2">Cover Details:</td></tr>
<tr><td>Start Date:</td><td>End Date:</td></tr>
</table>

<table>
<tr><td align="center">Notes</td></tr>
<tr><td></td></tr>
<tr><td></td></tr>
<tr><td></td></tr>
<tr><td></td></tr>
<tr><td></td></tr>
<tr><td></td></tr>
</table>

YEAR: ______ MONTH: ______ MODEL: ______

Date / Time	Oil Changed	Air Filter	Balance Tires	Wheel Alignment	Fuel Filter	Brakes Serviced	Spark Plugs	Transmission	Wiper Blades	Batteries	Radiator	Belts&Hoses	Mileage

make: _______________ date purchased: _______________

model: _______________ purchased price: _______________

license plate: _______________ purchased form: _______________

Date/Time	Maintenance/Comments	Mileage

Date/Time	Oil Changed	Air Filter	Balance Tires	Wheel Alignment	Fuel Filter	Brakes Serviced	Spark Plugs	Transmission	Wiper Blades	Batteries	Radiator	Belts&Horses	Mileage

make: _______________________   date purchased: _______________________

model: _______________________   purchased price: _______________________

license plate: _______________________   purchased form: _______________________

Date/Time	Maintenance/Comments	Mileage

YEAR: __________ MONTH: __________ MODEL: __________

Date / Time	Oil Changed	Air Filter	Balance Tires	Wheel Alignment	Fuel Filter	Brakes Serviced	Spark Plugs	Transmission	Wiper Blades	Batteries	Radiator	Belts&Hoses	Mileage

make: _______________________   date purchased: _______________________

model: _______________________   purchased price: _______________________

license plate: _______________________   purchased form: _______________________

Date/Time	Maintenance/Comments	Mileage

YEAR: ___________   MONTH: _________   MODEL: __________

Date / Time	Oil Changed	Air Filter	Balance Tires	Wheel Alignment	Fuel Filter	Brakes Serviced	Spark Plugs	Transmission	Wiper Blades	Batteries	Radiator	Belts&Hoses	Mileage

make: _______________________   date purchased: _______________________

model: _______________________   purchased price: _______________________

license plate: _______________________   purchased form: _______________________

Date/Time	Maintenance/Comments	Mileage

YEAR: _______ MONTH: _______ MODEL: _______

Date/Time	Oil Changed	Air Filter	Balance Tires	Wheel Alignment	Fuel Filter	Brakes Serviced	Spark Plugs	Transmission	Wiper Blades	Batteries	Radiator	Belts&Hoses	Mileage

make: _______________________   date purchased: _______________________

model: _______________________   purchased price: _______________________

license plate: _______________________   purchased form: _______________________

Date/Time	Maintenance/Comments	Mileage

YEAR: ______________ MONTH: ______________ MODEL: ______________

Date / Time	Oil Changed	Air Filter	Balance Tires	Wheel Alignment	Fuel Filter	Brakes Serviced	Spark Plugs	Transmission	Wiper Blades	Batteries	Radiator	Belts&Hoses	Mileage

make: _______________________   date purchased: _______________________

model: _______________________   purchased price: _______________________

license plate: _______________________   purchased form: _______________________

Date/Time	Maintenance/Comments	Mileage

YEAR: __________   MONTH: __________   MODEL: __________

Date / Time	Oil Changed	Air Filter	Balance Tires	Wheel Alignment	Fuel Filter	Brakes Serviced	Spark Plugs	Transmission	Wiper Blades	Batteries	Radiator	Belts&Hoses	Mileage

make: _______________________   date purchased: _______________________

model: _______________________   purchased price: _______________________

license plate: _______________________   purchased form: _______________________

Date/Time	Maintenance/Comments	Mileage

YEAR: __________ MONTH: __________ MODEL: __________

Date / Time	Oil Changed	Air Filter	Balance Tires	Wheel Alignment	Fuel Filter	Brakes Serviced	Spark Plugs	Transmission	Wiper Blades	Batteries	Radiator	Belts&Hoses	Mileage

make: _______________________   date purchased: _______________________

model: _______________________   purchased price: _______________________

license plate: _______________________   purchased form: _______________________

Date/Time	Maintenance/Comments	Mileage

YEAR: ___________ **MONTH:** ___________ **MODEL:** ___________

Date / Time	Oil Changed	Air Filter	Balance Tires	Wheel Alignment	Fuel Filter	Brakes Serviced	Spark Plugs	Transmission	Wiper Blades	Batteries	Radiator	Belts&Hoses	Mileage

make: ___________________________   date purchased: ___________________________

model: ___________________________   purchased price: ___________________________

license plate: ___________________________   purchased form: ___________________________

Date/Time	Maintenance/Comments	Mileage

YEAR: _________ MONTH: _________ MODEL: _________

Date / Time	Oil Changed	Air Filter	Balance Tires	Wheel Alignment	Fuel Filter	Brakes Serviced	Spark Plugs	Transmission	Wiper Blades	Batteries	Radiator	Belts&Hoses	Mileage

make: _______________________   date purchased: _______________

model: ______________________   purchased price: _______________

license plate: _______________   purchased form: _______________

Date/Time	Maintenance/Comments	Mileage

YEAR: _____________   MONTH: _____________   MODEL: _____________

Date / Time	Oil Changed	Air Filter	Balance Tires	Wheel Alignment	Fuel Filter	Brakes Serviced	Spark Plugs	Transmission	Wiper Blades	Batteries	Radiator	Belts&Hoses	Mileage

make: _______________________________

model: _______________________________

license plate: _______________________________

date purchased: _______________________________

purchased price: _______________________________

purchased form: _______________________________

Date/Time	Maintenance/Comments	Mileage

YEAR: ________	MONTH: ________	MODEL: ________

Date / Time	Oil Changed	Air Filter	Balance Tires	Wheel Alignment	Fuel Filter	Brakes Serviced	Spark Plugs	Transmission	Wiper Blades	Batteries	Radiator	Belts&Hoses	Mileage

make: _______________________   date purchased: _______________________

model: _______________________   purchased price: _______________________

license plate: _______________________   purchased form: _______________________

Date/Time	Maintenance/Comments	Mileage

| YEAR: __________ | MONTH: __________ | MODEL: __________ |

Date / Time	Oil Changed	Air Filter	Balance Tires	Wheel Alignment	Fuel Filter	Brakes Serviced	Spark Plugs	Transmission	Wiper Blades	Batteries	Radiator	Belts&Hoses	Mileage

make: date purchased:

model: purchased price:

license plate: purchased form:

Date/Time	Maintenance/Comments	Mileage

YEAR: _________   MONTH: _________   MODEL: _________

Date / Time	Oil Changed	Air Filter	Balance Tires	Wheel Alignment	Fuel Filter	Brakes Serviced	Spark Plugs	Transmission	Wiper Blades	Batteries	Radiator	Belts&Hoses	Mileage

make:

model:

license plate:

date purchased:

purchased price:

purchased form:

Date/Time	Maintenance/Comments	Mileage

Date / Time	Oil Changed	Air Filter	Balance Tires	Wheel Alignment	Fuel Filter	Brakes Serviced	Spark Plugs	Transmission	Wiper Blades	Batteries	Radiator	Belts&Hoses	Mileage

make: _______________________   date purchased: _______________________

model: _______________________   purchased price: _______________________

license plate: _______________________   purchased form: _______________________

Date/Time	Maintenance/Comments	Mileage

YEAR: _____________ MONTH: _____________ MODEL: _____________

Date / Time	Oil Changed	Air Filter	Balance Tires	Wheel Alignment	Fuel Filter	Brakes Serviced	Spark Plugs	Transmission	Wiper Blades	Batteries	Radiator	Belts&Hoses	Mileage

make: ___________________________ date purchased: ___________________

model: __________________________ purchased price: ___________________

license plate: ___________________ purchased form: ___________________

Date/Time	Maintenance/Comments	Mileage

YEAR: _________ MONTH: _________ MODEL: _________

Date/Time	Oil Changed	Air Filter	Balance Tires	Wheel Alignment	Fuel Filter	Brakes Serviced	Spark Plugs	Transmission	Wiper Blades	Batteries	Radiator	Belts&Hoses	Mileage

make: _______________________ date purchased: _______________________

model: _______________________ purchased price: _______________________

license plate: _______________________ purchased form: _______________________

Date/Time	Maintenance/Comments	Mileage

YEAR: ___________ MONTH: ___________ MODEL: ___________

Date / Time	Oil Changed	Air Filter	Balance Tires	Wheel Alignment	Fuel Filter	Brakes Serviced	Spark Plugs	Transmission	Wiper Blades	Batteries	Radiator	Belts&Hoses	Mileage

make: _______________________

model: _______________________

license plate: _______________________

date purchased: _______________________

purchased price: _______________________

purchased form: _______________________

Date/Time	Maintenance/Comments	Mileage

Date / Time	Oil Changed	Air Filter	Balance Tires	Wheel Alignment	Fuel Filter	Brakes Serviced	Spark Plugs	Transmission	Wiper Blades	Batteries	Radiator	Belts&Hoses	Mileage

make: ___________________   date purchased: ___________________

model: ___________________   purchased price: ___________________

license plate: ___________________   purchased form: ___________________

Date/Time	Maintenance/Comments	Mileage

YEAR: __________   MONTH: __________   MODEL: __________

Date / Time	Oil Changed	Air Filter	Balance Tires	Wheel Alignment	Fuel Filter	Brakes Serviced	Spark Plugs	Transmission	Wiper Blades	Batteries	Radiator	Belts&Hoses	Mileage

make: _______________________   date purchased: _______________________

model: _______________________   purchased price: _______________________

license plate: _______________________   purchased form: _______________________

Date/Time	Maintenance/Comments	Mileage

YEAR: _______ MONTH: _______ MODEL: _______

Date / Time	Oil Changed	Air Filter	Balance Tires	Wheel Alignment	Fuel Filter	Brakes Serviced	Spark Plugs	Transmission	Wiper Blades	Batteries	Radiator	Belts&Horses	Mileage

make: ___________________________

model: ___________________________

license plate: ___________________________

date purchased: ___________________________

purchased price: ___________________________

purchased form: ___________________________

DATE/TIME	MAINTENANCE/COMMENTS	MILEAGE

YEAR: __________   MONTH: __________   MODEL: __________

Date / Time	Oil Changed	Air Filter	Balance Tires	Wheel Alignment	Fuel Filter	Brakes Serviced	Spark Plugs	Transmission	Wiper Blades	Batteries	Radiator	Belts&Hoses	Mileage

make: _______________________

model: _______________________

license plate: _______________________

date purchased: _______________________

purchased price: _______________________

purchased form: _______________________

Date/Time	Maintenance/Comments	Mileage

Date / Time	Oil Changed	Air Filter	Balance Tires	Wheel Alignment	Fuel Filter	Brakes Serviced	Spark Plugs	Transmission	Wiper Blades	Batteries	Radiator	Belts&Hoses	Mileage

make: _______________________   date purchased: _______________________

model: _______________________   purchased price: _______________________

license plate: _______________________   purchased form: _______________________

Date/Time	Maintenance/Comments	Mileage

YEAR: __________ MONTH: __________ MODEL: __________

Date / Time	Oil Changed	Air Filter	Balance Tires	Wheel Alignment	Fuel Filter	Brakes Serviced	Spark Plugs	Transmission	Wiper Blades	Batteries	Radiator	Belts&Hoses	Mileage

make: _______________________________

model: _______________________________

license plate: _______________________________

date purchased: _______________________________

purchased price: _______________________________

purchased form: _______________________________

Date/Time	Maintenance/Comments	Mileage

<table>
<tr><td></td><td>YEAR: _______</td><td>MONTH: _______</td><td>MODEL: _______</td></tr>
</table>

Date / Time	Oil Changed	Air Filter	Balance Tires	Wheel Alignment	Fuel Filter	Brakes Serviced	Spark Plugs	Transmission	Wiper Blades	Batteries	Radiator	Belts&Hoses	Mileage

make: _______________________   date purchased: _______________________

model: _______________________   purchased price: _______________________

license plate: _______________________   purchased form: _______________________

Date/Time	Maintenance/Comments	Mileage

YEAR: __________ MONTH: __________ MODEL: __________

Date / Time	Oil Changed	Air Filter	Balance Tires	Wheel Alignment	Fuel Filter	Brakes Serviced	Spark Plugs	Transmission	Wiper Blades	Batteries	Radiator	Belts&Hoses	Mileage

make: _______________________   date purchased: _______________________

model: _______________________   purchased price: _______________________

license plate: _______________________   purchased form: _______________________

Date/Time	Maintenance/Comments	Mileage

<table>
<tr><td rowspan="2">YEAR: __________</td><td>MONTH: __________</td><td>MODEL: __________</td></tr>
</table>

Date / Time	Oil Changed	Air Filter	Balance Tires	Wheel Alignment	Fuel Filter	Brakes Serviced	Spark Plugs	Transmission	Wiper Blades	Batteries	Radiator	Belts&Hoses	Mileage

make: _______________________

model: _______________________

license plate: _______________________

date purchased: _______________________

purchased price: _______________________

purchased form: _______________________

Date/Time	Maintenance/Comments	Mileage

YEAR: _________ MONTH: _________ MODEL: _________

Date / Time	Oil Changed	Air Filter	Balance Tires	Wheel Alignment	Fuel Filter	Brakes Serviced	Spark Plugs	Transmission	Wiper Blades	Batteries	Radiator	Belts&Hoses	Mileage

make:

date purchased:

model:

purchased price:

license plate:

purchased form:

Date/Time	Maintenance/Comments	Mileage

YEAR: ____________ MONTH: ____________ MODEL: ____________

Date / Time	Oil Changed	Air Filter	Balance Tires	Wheel Alignment	Fuel Filter	Brakes Serviced	Spark Plugs	Transmission	Wiper Blades	Batteries	Radiator	Belts&Hoses	Mileage

make: _______________________ date purchased: _______________________

model: _______________________ purchased price: _______________________

license plate: _______________________ purchased form: _______________________

Date/Time	Maintenance/Comments	Mileage

Date / Time	Oil Changed	Air Filter	Balance Tires	Wheel Alignment	Fuel Filter	Brakes Serviced	Spark Plugs	Transmission	Wiper Blades	Batteries	Radiator	Belts & Hoses	Mileage

make: ____   date purchased: _____________________________

model: _____________________________________   purchased price: ____________________________

license plate: _________________________________   purchased form: ____________________________

DATE/TIME	MAINTENANCE/COMMENTS	MILEAGE

Date / Time	Oil Changed	Air Filter	Balance Tires	Wheel Alignment	Fuel Filter	Brakes Serviced	Spark Plugs	Transmission	Wiper Blades	Batteries	Radiator	Belts&Hoses	Mileage

make: _______________________   date purchased: _______________________

model: _______________________   purchased price: _______________________

license plate: _______________________   purchased form: _______________________

Date/Time	Maintenance/Comments	Mileage

YEAR: _________ MONTH: _________ MODEL: _________

Date / Time	Oil Changed	Air Filter	Balance Tires	Wheel Alignment	Fuel Filter	Brakes Serviced	Spark Plugs	Transmission	Wiper Blades	Batteries	Radiator	Belts&Hoses	Mileage

make: _______________________   date purchased: _______________________

model: _______________________   purchased price: _______________________

license plate: _______________________   purchased form: _______________________

Date/Time	Maintenance/Comments	Mileage

YEAR: _______   **MONTH:** _______   **MODEL:** _______

Date / Time	Oil Changed	Air Filter	Balance Tires	Wheel Alignment	Fuel Filter	Brakes Serviced	Spark Plugs	Transmission	Wiper Blades	Batteries	Radiator	Belts&Hoses	Mileage

make: _______________________   date purchased: _______________________

model: _______________________   purchased price: _______________________

license plate: _______________________   purchased form: _______________________

Date/Time	Maintenance/Comments	Mileage

YEAR: __________   MONTH: __________   MODEL: __________

Date / Time	Oil Changed	Air Filter	Balance Tires	Wheel Alignment	Fuel Filter	Brakes Serviced	Spark Plugs	Transmission	Wiper Blades	Batteries	Radiator	Belts&Hoses	Mileage

make: ______________________________   date purchased: ______________________________

model: ______________________________   purchased price: ______________________________

license plate: ______________________________   purchased form: ______________________________

Date/Time	Maintenance/Comments	Mileage

YEAR: _________   MONTH: _________   MODEL: _________

Date / Time	Oil Changed	Air Filter	Balance Tires	Wheel Alignment	Fuel Filter	Brakes Serviced	Spark Plugs	Transmission	Wiper Blades	Batteries	Radiator	Belts&Horses	Mileage

make: ___________________________   date purchased: ___________________________

model: ___________________________   purchased price: ___________________________

license plate: ___________________________   purchased form: ___________________________

Date/Time	Maintenance/Comments	Mileage

YEAR: _________ MONTH: _________ MODEL: _________

Date / Time	Oil Changed	Air Filter	Balance Tires	Wheel Alignment	Fuel Filter	Brakes Serviced	Spark Plugs	Transmission	Wiper Blades	Batteries	Radiator	Belts&Horses	Mileage

make: _______________________   date purchased: _______________________

model: _______________________   purchased price: _______________________

license plate: _______________________   purchased form: _______________________

Date/Time	Maintenance/Comments	Mileage

Date / Time	Oil Changed	Air Filter	Balance Tires	Wheel Alignment	Fuel Filter	Brakes Serviced	Spark Plugs	Transmission	Wiper Blades	Batteries	Radiator	Belts&Hoses	Mileage

make: _________________________ date purchased: _________________________

model: _________________________ purchased price: _________________________

license plate: _________________________ purchased form: _________________________

Date/Time	Maintenance/Comments	Mileage

YEAR: _________ MONTH: _________ MODEL: _________

Date / Time	Oil Changed	Air Filter	Balance Tires	Wheel Alignment	Fuel Filter	Brakes Serviced	Spark Plugs	Transmission	Wiper Blades	Batteries	Radiator	Belts&Hoses	Mileage

make: _____________________   date purchased: _____________________

model: _____________________   purchased price: _____________________

license plate: _____________________   purchased form: _____________________

Date/Time	Maintenance/Comments	Mileage

YEAR: __________ MONTH: __________ MODEL: __________

Date / Time	Oil Changed	Air Filter	Balance Tires	Wheel Alignment	Fuel Filter	Brakes Serviced	Spark Plugs	Transmission	Wiper Blades	Batteries	Radiator	Belts&Hoses	Mileage

make: _____________________ date purchased: _____________________

model: _____________________ purchased price: _____________________

license plate: _____________________ purchased form: _____________________

Date/Time	Maintenance/Comments	Mileage

Date / Time	Oil Changed	Air Filter	Balance Tires	Wheel Alignment	Fuel Filter	Brakes Serviced	Spark Plugs	Transmission	Wiper Blades	Batteries	Radiator	Belts&Hoses	Mileage

make: ______________________________   date purchased: ______________________________

model: ______________________________   purchased price: ______________________________

license plate: ______________________________   purchased form: ______________________________

Date/Time	Maintenance/Comments	Mileage

YEAR: _________   MONTH: _________   MODEL: _________

Date / Time	Oil Changed	Air Filter	Balance Tires	Wheel Alignment	Fuel Filter	Brakes Serviced	Spark Plugs	Transmission	Wiper Blades	Batteries	Radiator	Belts&Hoses	Mileage

make: date purchased:

model: purchased price:

license plate: purchased form:

DATE/TIME	MAINTENANCE/COMMENTS	MILEAGE

Date / Time	Oil Changed	Air Filter	Balance Tires	Wheel Alignment	Fuel Filter	Brakes Serviced	Spark Plugs	Transmission	Wiper Blades	Batteries	Radiator	Belts&Horses	Mileage

make: _______________________ date purchased: _______________________

model: ______________________ purchased price: _______________________

license plate: ______________ purchased form: _______________________

Date/Time	Maintenance/Comments	Mileage

<table>
<tr><td rowspan="2">Date / Time</td><td>Oil Changed</td><td>Air Filter</td><td>Balance Tires</td><td>Wheel Alignment</td><td>Fuel Filter</td><td>Brakes Serviced</td><td>Spark Plugs</td><td>Transmission</td><td>Wiper Blades</td><td>Batteries</td><td>Radiator</td><td>Belts&Hoses</td><td rowspan="2">Mileage</td></tr>
<tr><td></td><td></td><td></td><td></td><td></td><td></td><td></td><td></td><td></td><td></td><td></td><td></td></tr>
</table>

YEAR: ________ **MONTH:** ________ **MODEL:** ________

make:

model:

license plate:

date purchased:

purchased price:

purchased form:

Date/Time	Maintenance/Comments	Mileage

YEAR: _________ MONTH: _________ MODEL: _________

Date / Time	Oil Changed	Air Filter	Balance Tires	Wheel Alignment	Fuel Filter	Brakes Serviced	Spark Plugs	Transmission	Wiper Blades	Batteries	Radiator	Belts&Hoses	Mileage

make: date purchased:

model: purchased price:

license plate: purchased form:

Date/Time	Maintenance/Comments	Mileage

YEAR: __________ **MONTH:** __________ **MODEL:** __________

Date / Time	Oil Changed	Air Filter	Balance Tires	Wheel Alignment	Fuel Filter	Brakes Serviced	Spark Plugs	Transmission	Wiper Blades	Batteries	Radiator	Belts&Hoses	Mileage

make:		date purchased:
model:		purchased price:
license plate:		purchased form:

Date/Time	Maintenance/Comments	Mileage

YEAR: ___________ **MONTH:** ___________ **MODEL:** ___________

Date / Time	Oil Changed	Air Filter	Balance Tires	Wheel Alignment	Fuel Filter	Brakes Serviced	Spark Plugs	Transmission	Wiper Blades	Batteries	Radiator	Belts&Hoses	Mileage

make:

date purchased:

model:

purchased price:

license plate:

purchased form:

Date/Time	Maintenance/Comments	Mileage

YEAR: _________   MONTH: _________   MODEL: _________

Date / Time	Oil Changed	Air Filter	Balance Tires	Wheel Alignment	Fuel Filter	Brakes Serviced	Spark Plugs	Transmission	Wiper Blades	Batteries	Radiator	Belts&Hoses	Mileage

YEARLY SUMMARY

month	total distance	total cost of fuel	total repairs	total maint.
jan				
feb				
mar				
apr				
may				
jun				
jul				
aug				
sep				
oct				
nov				
dec				

Thank you!

WE ARE GLAD THAT YOU PURCHASED OUR BOOK!
PLEASE LET US KNOW HOW WE CAN IMPROVE IT!
YOUR FEEDBACK IS ESSENTIAL TO US.

Contact us at:

 log'Sin@gmail.com

---

JUST TITLE THE EMAIL 'CREATIVE' AND WE WILL

GIVE YOU SOME EXTRA SURPRISES!

www.ingramcontent.com/pod-product-compliance
Lightning Source LLC
LaVergne TN
LVHW011038200726
843509LV00011B/1310